OUR
GRE★T
STATES

WHAT'S GREAT ABOUT
# CONNECTICUT?

✳ Rebecca Rissman

LERNER PUBLICATIONS ✳ MINNEAPOLIS

# CONTENTS

Content Consultant: Tom Ratliff, History Professor, Central Connecticut State University

Lerner Publications Company
A division of Lerner Publishing Group, Inc.
241 First Avenue North
Minneapolis, MN 55401 USA

For reading levels and more information, look up this title at www.lernerbooks.com.

Main body text set in ITC Franklin Gothic Std Book Condensed 12/15.
Typeface provided by Adobe Systems.

Library of Congress Cataloging-in-Publication Data
Rissman, Rebecca.
    What's great about Connecticut? / by Rebecca Rissman.
        pages    cm. — (Our great states)
    Includes index.
    ISBN 978-1-4677-3857-6 (lib. bdg. : alk. paper)
    ISBN 978-1-4677-6081-2 (pbk.)
    ISBN 978-1-4677-6259-5 (EB pdf)
    1.  Connecticut—Juvenile literature.
I. Title.
F94.3.R57 2015
974.6—dc23                          2014026781

Manufactured in the United States of America
1 - PC - 12/31/14

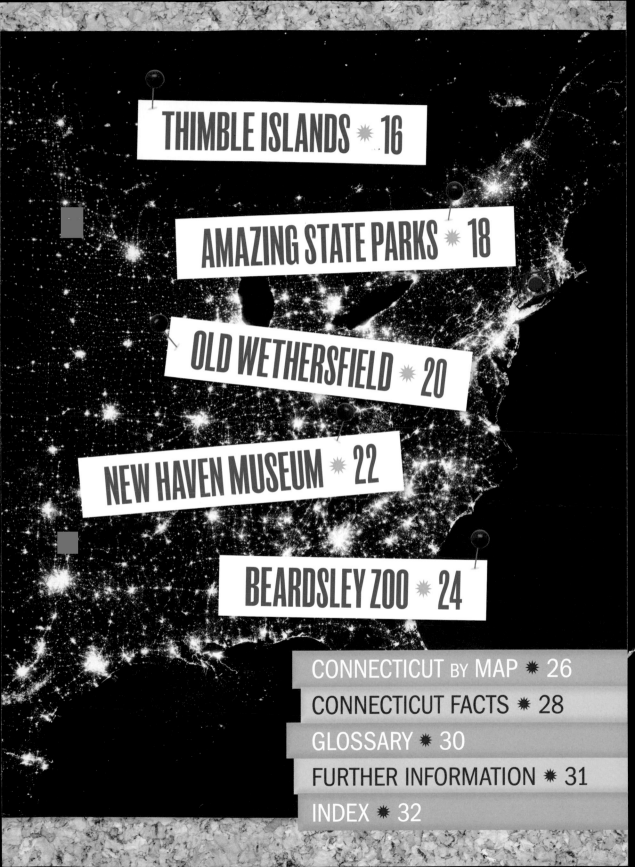

# CONNECTICUT Welcomes You!

Are you ready for an adventure? Head to Connecticut! You'll watch the past come alive in the historic villages. Enjoy the outdoors at Long Island Sound or Thimble Islands. Or maybe you'd like to explore one of the state's parks. Put on your hiking boots and tour beautiful hills and waterfalls. Enjoy a sunny day at the beach in the summer, or ski during the winter. Connecticut may be a small state, but it's full of amazing places to see. Keep reading to learn about the top ten places to visit!

Mount Frissell
(2,380 feet/
725 m)

MASSACHUSETTS

NEW YORK

West Hartford

Hartford

Bristol

New Britain

Naugatuck River

Housatonic River

Waterbury

Meriden

Connecticut River

Quinebaug River

RHODE ISLAND

Miles
0     5     10     15
0   5   10   15   20
Kilometers

N

Danbury

New Haven

Bridgeport

Norwalk

Stamford

Long Island Sound

Explore Connecticut's parks and all the places in between! Just turn the page to find out about the CONSTITUTION STATE. >

This dome has been built over the open fossil pit at Dinosaur State Park.

# DINOSAUR TRACKS!

THE TRACKWAY

> You'll want to make your first Connecticut stop at Dinosaur State Park in Rocky Hill. See where dinosaurs wandered prehistoric Connecticut. The park is home to a collection of 200-million-year-old fossils. Watch a short video that shows how the dinosaur tracks formed. Then see how many different tracks you can find!

Be sure to visit the dinosaur track-casting station. You can help make a cast of a dinosaur footprint. This is part of what paleontologists do when they work. Pour plaster into one of the footprints. Wait until the plaster is dry, and then pull it out. Now you have a handmade souvenir: a mold of a real dinosaur's footprint!

After you've washed the plaster off your hands, head to the Discovery Room. Touch real fossils from around the world. Then explore the 2.5 miles (4 kilometers) of trails outside. You'll see many plants and animals along the way.

## LAND FORMATIONS

Prehistoric Connecticut was covered in mountains. Over the years, glaciers and erosion wore them down. Now the state is covered in hills and valleys. The glaciers and the erosion also revealed ancient fossils. Many of the dinosaur fossils found in Connecticut were uncovered in the Connecticut River valley.

# MASHANTUCKET PEQUOT MUSEUM

> Travel back in time at the Mashantucket Pequot Museum. This museum in the town of Mashantucket is full of American Indian history. Take in the sights and sounds from the Pequot nation.

Start your museum tour in the World of Ice exhibits. You'll feel as if you've stepped into a glacier. Listen to and feel the icy wind. Beavers, wolves, and wooly mammoths are a few of the models of animals you may see. Then learn how Pequot families hunted caribou more than six thousand years ago.

It's time to warm up! Wander through a Pequot village. Here you'll find wigwams and clothing on display that is just like what you would've seen in a Pequot village in the 1500s. Enjoy the shade of the trees and smell the smoky campfires. You'll hear the sounds of a busy American Indian community. End your visit with a snack from the café. Or maybe you'd like to stop in the gift shop for a souvenir.

See displays such as this mealtime scene at the Mashantucket Pequot Museum.

## AMERICAN INDIAN NAMES

Many groups of American Indians lived in Connecticut before European settlers arrived in the 1600s. The word *Connecticut* comes from the Algonquin word *quinnitukqut*. This means "long river place" or "beside the long tidal river." The name refers to the Connecticut River.

# CONNECTICUT
# SCIENCE CENTER

> Be sure to check out the Connecticut Science Center in downtown Hartford. You'll enjoy a day of adventure, technology, and fun!

Get ready to blast off in the Exploring Space exhibit. Strap into your very own flight chair. You'll experience what life might be like if you were an astronaut. Then take over the controls of the simulator and fly over Mars. You can even explore a black hole. When you're done in the flight chair, check out some moon rocks.

After exploring space, make your way to the Sports Lab. Take a quiz to see what sport fits your personality best. The quiz will even tell you how to get involved! You'll also learn the importance of proper sports equipment. Build your own helmet using padding.

If you're visiting the Connecticut Science Center on a nice day, check out the museum's rooftop garden. It overlooks the Connecticut River.

You can make—and then test—your own helmet using a test dummy and a small wrecking ball in the Sports Lab exhibit.

# THE MARK TWAIN HOUSE & MUSEUM

> Continue exploring Hartford by stopping at the Mark Twain House & Museum. The great American author Samuel Clemens lived in this house from 1874 to 1891. You may know Clemens as Mark Twain, which was his pen name. Some of Twain's most famous books include *The Adventures of Tom Sawyer* and *The Adventures of Huckleberry Finn.* Twain wrote these books in this twenty-five-room mansion.

Sign up for a guided tour of the mansion. Your tour guide will tell you stories of Twain and his family as you walk through the house. Pick your favorite room. Maybe it's the drawing room or the library! After walking through the house, stop in the museum. Here you'll learn more about Twain's life and writing. Be sure to watch the short film about Twain too.

If you're feeling brave enough, check out one of the Graveyard Shift Ghost Tours. These nighttime tours feature spooky stories, fascinating facts, and sometimes even ghost sightings!

Mark Twain (*left*) helped design his family's Hartford home (*below*), which is open to visitors.

# MYSTIC SEAPORT

> If you're looking to spend time on the water, stop in Mystic. This town borders a body of water called the Long Island Sound. This estuary separates Connecticut from Long Island, part of New York. Mystic has sandy beaches, and the water in the sound is calm. It is a great place to fish, sail, and explore.

If you're ready for adventure, visit Mystic Seaport: The Museum of America and the Sea. Here you can see boats on display. Climb aboard a whaling vessel. You'll learn about the history of whale hunting. Or set sail on a 1908 coal-powered steamboat. Pretend you are a sea captain. You can also pretend to sail a historic yacht.

Check out the Children's Museum. You'll help clean the deck of a ship and move cargo. You can even try on a sailor's outfit.

End your visit by wandering through an 1800s seaside village. Stop at the ship carver's shop. The carver makes wooden carvings that appear on ships. You can also stop at the tavern for a snack. Or maybe you'd like to walk through the gardens. To see the whole village, take a horse-drawn carriage ride.

## LONG ISLAND SOUND

Long Island Sound is important to Connecticut's economy. The state makes approximately $5.5 billion from Long Island Sound tourism each year. These activities include fishing, swimming, and boating.

ROANN

L.A. DUNTON

Before you leave Mystic Seaport: The Museum of America and the Sea, see where the captain used to sleep on the whaling vessel.

# THIMBLE ISLANDS

> Hop in the car and drive approximately an hour west from Mystic to Thimble Islands. Roll the windows down and smell the salty sea air! Then board a ferry. Listen to the captain's stories as he sails the boat around the islands.

Thimble Islands is made up of hundreds of small islands. They are found in the Long Island Sound. Some islands are rocky and bare. Others are covered in thick forest. And some are only above water when the tide is low!

Try exploring an island from a kayak. Put on a life jacket and slather on some sunscreen. The waters are usually calm. Splash, race, and swim!

When you need a break, pull ashore onto a peaceful beach. Take some time to relax in the sunshine. Or find a dock for some fishing. Look up in the sky and see if you can spot some of Connecticut's beautiful birds. Seagulls, herons, and loons are just a few birds you may see.

Herons are common birds to see near Thimble Islands.

## BURIED TREASURE!

Thimble Islands have an important place in Connecticut's history and economy. In the 1840s, one island's owner said a famous pirate, Captain William Kidd, buried treasure on the islands. This wasn't true. But people rushed to the islands in search of treasure. The islands are still a popular place for tourists. But no one has found any buried treasure.

Captain Kidd

17

# AMAZING STATE PARKS

> Put on your hiking boots. It's time to hit the trails! Connecticut has many state parks full of natural wonders.

You'll want to visit Sleeping Giant State Park in Hamden. Hike, climb, and ride through this historic and beautiful rock formation. Even if you don't agree that the mountain looks like a giant, you'll enjoy the view from the top! Long Island Sound and New Haven can be seen from here.

During the summer months, explore the hiking trails on horseback or on foot. You may see foxes or deer. Or maybe you'll see lizards or snakes. Strap on cross-country skis in the winter. You'll enjoy a chilly day in nature.

After visiting Sleeping Giant, drive approximately one hour to Kent Falls State Park. Listen for the roar of Kent Falls. This area is one of the state's most popular places to visit. Remember to pack a raincoat. Water blows onto nearby hikers. Pack a picnic to enjoy at the falls. Then try fishing for trout in the river. Perhaps you'll catch a big one!

American Indians gave Sleeping Giant Mountain its name because they believed it looked like a sleeping giant.

Snowshoeing is a fun activity to enjoy at Sleeping Giant State Park.

# OLD WETHERSFIELD

> Make your next stop the Webb-Deane-Stevens Museum in Wethersfield. The museum is named after colonists and diplomats from the mid-1700s. You can experience life during the American Revolution (1775–1783).

Find a seat and watch as soldiers on horseback ride into battle. Actors reenact the battle. They also show how to use historic weapons. You may see a musket being fired. Talk to the soldiers after the battle is over. You can ask them about life during the war.

Sign up for an hour-long tour. It will take you through four historic homes. See colonial furniture. Your guide will tell you stories about the buildings. Can you find the house George Washington used? He stayed in the Webb House for five days in 1781. Be sure to walk through the colonial garden too.

Actors dressed up as 1700s colonists are a common sight at the Webb-Deane-Stevens Museum.

## STATE SONG

The American Revolution was fought between American colonists and Great Britain. During the war, British soldiers often made fun of Americans by singing a song called "Yankee Doodle." Many stories say the colonists adopted the song after winning a battle against the British. It was a way of letting the British know they had been defeated. The song eventually became the state song of Connecticut!

# NEW HAVEN MUSEUM

See actors dressed as colonists doing chores at the New Haven Museum.

> New Haven is a busy modern city. But in the 1600s, it was a very different place. Connecticut became an English colony in 1635. At the New Haven Museum, you'll learn about the brave settlers' lives.

The ocean was very important to early settlers. Visit the Sailors, Ships & Sea Captains exhibit. You can meet an actor playing a historic sea captain. Feel free to ask him about his life, his work, and the dangers he faced. Then learn how to pack for a long sea voyage. How many pairs of socks do you think you'd need?

After talking to the captain, make your way to the Growing Up in the 1700s program. Learn all about how colonial kids lived.

Make your final stop the Pardee-Morris House. The British burned this 1700s farmhouse during a raid in 1779. The Morris family rebuilt the home and kept the house in the family until the early 1900s. Take a tour of the house or catch a concert on the front lawn during the summer.

PARDEE~
MORRIS
HOUSE:

BURNED JULY 5, 1779
DURING A BRITISH RAID
REBUILT 1780

A PROPERTY OF
THE NEW HAVEN COLONY
HISTORICAL SOCIETY

# BEARDSLEY ZOO

> If you're looking to spend some time with animals, head to the Beardsley Zoo in Bridgeport. You can explore a South American rain forest without ever leaving Connecticut! You'll see monkeys and bats in the rain forest building.

Heads up! Watch for low-flying birds as you walk through the zoo. They fly freely in the bird exhibit. Try to spot a blue-and-gold macaw and a black swan. You may even see a green heron, a redhead duck, or a white-lined tanager. It's a rainbow of birds!

Wander through the prairie dog exhibit. Watch for these playful critters as they run in and out of their many tunnels. Don't forget to walk by the sheep and the bison.

If you're getting hungry, grab a snack at the Peacock Café. It's right by the tigers, the leopards, and the lynx. Don't forget to say hi to those animals. Each tiger at this zoo eats the equivalent of 161 steaks each week!

This book includes a list of ten amazing Connecticut attractions. If you could plan your own trip to Connecticut, what ten sights and things to do would you want it to include? Think about the subjects, activities, and foods you most enjoy. Draw your own map of the state and create your ideal trip route, putting stars on the attractions you want to see and adding a dotted line between them all.

Lynx and peacocks are just a few of the animals you'll see at the Beardsley Zoo!

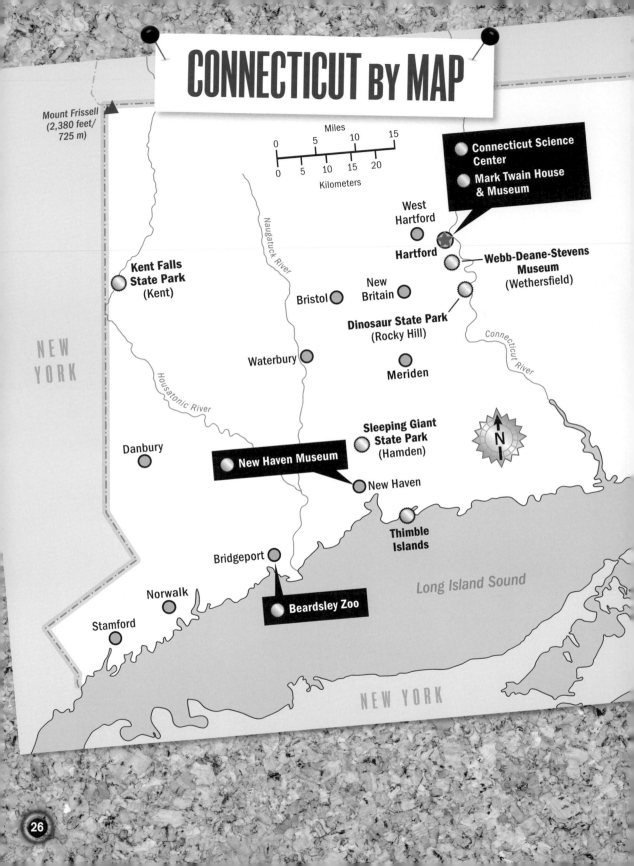

# CONNECTICUT BY MAP

Mount Frissell
(2,380 feet/
725 m)

**Miles**
0    5    10    15

**Kilometers**
0    5    10    15    20

Connecticut Science Center

Mark Twain House & Museum

West Hartford

Hartford

Webb-Deane-Stevens Museum (Wethersfield)

Kent Falls State Park (Kent)

Bristol

New Britain

Dinosaur State Park (Rocky Hill)

NEW YORK

Waterbury

Meriden

Danbury

Sleeping Giant State Park (Hamden)

New Haven Museum

New Haven

Naugatuck River

Housatonic River

Connecticut River

N

Thimble Islands

Bridgeport

Long Island Sound

Beardsley Zoo

Norwalk

Stamford

NEW YORK

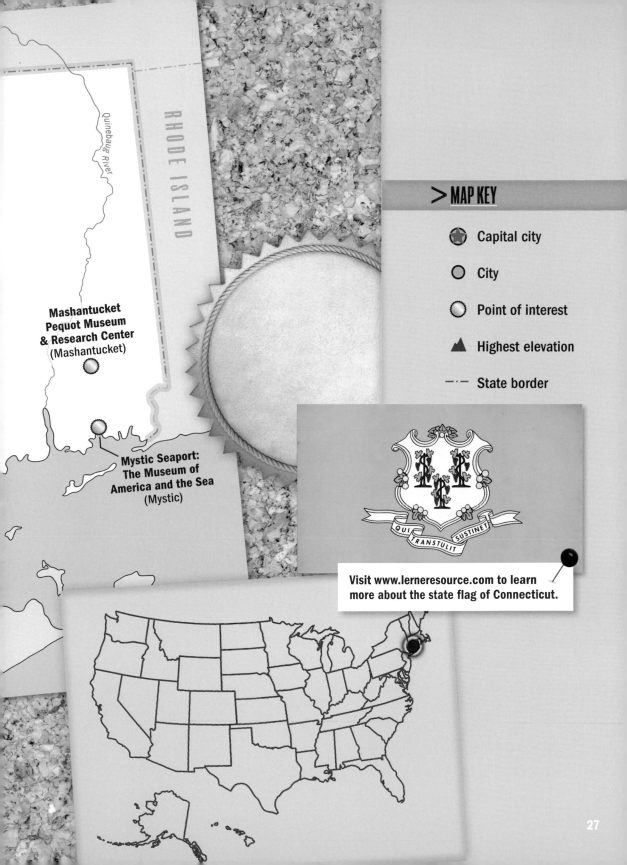

RHODE ISLAND

Quinebaug River

**Mashantucket Pequot Museum & Research Center**
(Mashantucket)

**Mystic Seaport: The Museum of America and the Sea**
(Mystic)

Visit www.lerneresource.com to learn more about the state flag of Connecticut.

## > MAP KEY

⬟ Capital city

◯ City

◉ Point of interest

▲ Highest elevation

–·– State border

QUI TRANSTULIT SUSTINET

# CONNECTICUT FACTS

**NICKNAME:** The Constitution State

**SONG:** "Yankee Doodle"

**MOTTO:** *Qui transtulit sustinet*, or "He who transplanted still sustains"

> **FLOWER:** mountain laurel

**TREE:** white oak

> **BIRD:** American robin

**ANIMAL:** sperm whale

**DATE AND RANK OF STATEHOOD:** January 9, 1788; the 5th state

> **CAPITAL:** Hartford

**AREA:** 5,004 square miles (12,960 sq. km)

**AVERAGE JANUARY TEMPERATURE:** 26°F (–3°C)

**AVERAGE JULY TEMPERATURE:** 71°F (22°C)

**POPULATION AND RANK:** 3,596,080; 29th (2013)

**MAJOR CITIES AND POPULATIONS:** Bridgeport (144,229), New Haven (129,779), Hartford (125,017), Stamford (122,643), Waterbury (110,366)

**NUMBER OF US CONGRESS MEMBERS:** 5 representatives, 2 senators

**NUMBER OF ELECTORAL VOTES:** 7

**NATURAL RESOURCES:** clay, granite, limestone

> **AGRICULTURAL PRODUCTS:** eggs, greenhouse and nursery products, milk, apples

**MANUFACTURED GOODS:** chemicals, computer and electronic products, electrical equipment, machinery

# GLOSSARY

**cast:** a shape created from liquid hardening in a mold

**estuary:** the tidal mouth of a large river

**glacier:** a giant piece of ice that slowly moves across the land

**musket:** a historic type of gun

**paleontologist:** a scientist who works with fossils of animals and plants that lived long ago

**prehistoric:** existing in the time before people could write

**sound:** a narrow area of water that connects two bodies of water, or that forms an inlet

**souvenir:** something to keep as a reminder of a place you visited

**whaling:** the practice of hunting for whales

**wigwam:** a type of home made by North American Indians

**yacht:** a large boat

# FURTHER INFORMATION

Bross, Tom, and Joan Bross. *Connecticut Off the Beaten Path.* 8th ed. Guilford, CT: Morris Book Publishing, 2009. Read this book to learn about some of Connecticut's lesser-known sights.

Burgan, Michael. *It's My State: Connecticut.* New York: Marshall Cavendish, 2010. Read this book to learn all about the history, the people, and the landforms of Connecticut.

**Connecticut Wildlife**
http://www.wildlifeofct.com
If you like learning about wild animals in Connecticut, check out this site to learn more.

**ConneCT Kids**
http://www.kids.ct.gov/kids/site/default.asp
Check out this kid-friendly site to learn all about Connecticut.

**50States**
http://www.50states.com/connecti.htm#.VBdb97Eo6Uk
Head to this handy website for quick information on Connecticut and any other state you're interested in.

Savage, Jeff. *Maya Moore*. Minneapolis: Lerner Publications, 2012. Moore won multiple NCAA basketball championships with the University of Connecticut.

# INDEX

## PHOTO ACKNOWLEDGMENTS

The images in this book are used with the permission of: © Enfi/Shutterstock Images, pp. 1, 4–5; NASA, pp. 2–3; © Thinkstock, p. 4; © Laura Westlund/Independent Picture Service, pp. 5, 26–27; © George Ruhe/AP Images, pp. 6–7; © Jeffrey M. Frank/Shutterstock Images, p. 6; © drewthehobbit/Shutterstock Images, p. 7; © Andre Jenny Stock Connection Worldwide/Newscom, pp. 8–9; © Randy Duchaine/Alamy, pp. 9 (top), 10–11; Library of Congress, pp. 9 (bottom) (LC-USF34-080967-E), 15 (top) (LC-DIG-highsm-19011), 16–17 (LC-DIG-highsm-18915), 29 (bottom right) (LC-DIG-highsm-18822); © Laura Stone/Shutterstock Images, p. 11 (left); Vilseskogen/Flickr, p. 11 (right); © Hemis/Zuma Press/Newscom, pp. 12–13; Mathew Brady, p. 13 (left); © Thinkstock, p. 13 (right); © Donald Gargano/Shutterstock Images, pp. 14–15, 15 (bottom); © Joseph Scott Photography/Shutterstock Images, p. 17 (top); Public Domain, pp. 17 (bottom), 21 (right); © Richard Cavalleri/Shutterstock Images, pp. 18–19; © Enigma/Alamy, p. 19 (left); © Alfaguarilla/Shutterstock Images, p. 19 (right); © Stephen Saks Photography/Alamy, pp. 20–21; © Stan Tess/Alamy, pp. 21 (left), 22; © Bob Child/AP Images, pp. 22–23; © S. Cooper Digital/Shutterstock Images, pp. 24–25; © Chase Clausen/Shutterstock Images, p. 25 (right); © Volodymyr Burdiak/Shutterstock Images, p. 25 (left); © nicoolay/iStockphoto, p. 27; © Melinda Fawver/Shutterstock Images, p. 29 (top right); © David Spates/Shutterstock Images, p. 29 (top left); © Sea Wave/Shutterstock Images, p. 29 (bottom left).

Cover: © Rudi Von Briel/Getty Images (ship); © Michael Melford/National Geographic/Getty Images (whale); © iStockphoto.com/kbwillis (waterfall); © Laura Westlund/Independent Picture Service (map); © iStockphoto.com/fpm (seal); © iStockphoto.com/vicm (pushpins); © iStockphoto.com/benz190 (corkboard).